Holly

Yew

Jackfruit

Kapok

Crepe myrtle

European larch

Walnut

Published by
Princeton Architectural Press
70 West 36th Street
New York, New York 10018
www.papress.com

Printed and bound in China
24 23 22   4 3 2
Originally published in French as *Le Livre aux Arbres*
© Editions Belin / Humensis, 2020
Translated from the French by Yolanda Stern Broad

ISBN 978-1-61689-971-4

Library of Congress Cataloging-in-Publication Data available upon request.

Nathalie Tordjman

THE BOOK OF AMAZING TREES

illustrated by

Julien Norwood & Isabelle Simler

Princeton Architectural Press · New York

Contents

THE BIRTH OF A TREE

INTRODUCING THE TREES

AMAZING PLANTS

>>>—<<<

Trees are plants that tower high in the sky.

5 characteristics of trees

* They grow a single stem, called a **trunk**, which can become very thick, and they have branches.
* They make a solid material: **lignin**, the main component of wood.
* They grow and spend their entire lives in the same place, attached to the ground by their **roots**.
* They can live for several decades: they are **perennial plants**.
* They bear **flowers** and **fruit**.

These plants are not trees!

Palm tree
It doesn't have any branches, and what looks like a trunk is what is left of its withered leaves.

Bamboo
It doesn't have any branches, and its stem is hollow.

Trees grow in every size!

A subshrub

Heather

It measures less than 3 feet (1 m) high.

A small shrub

Gorse

It measures 13 to 16.5 feet (4 to 5 m) high.

A large shrub

Hazelnut tree

It measures 19.5 to 26 feet (6 to 8 m) high.

A tree in detail

An English oak

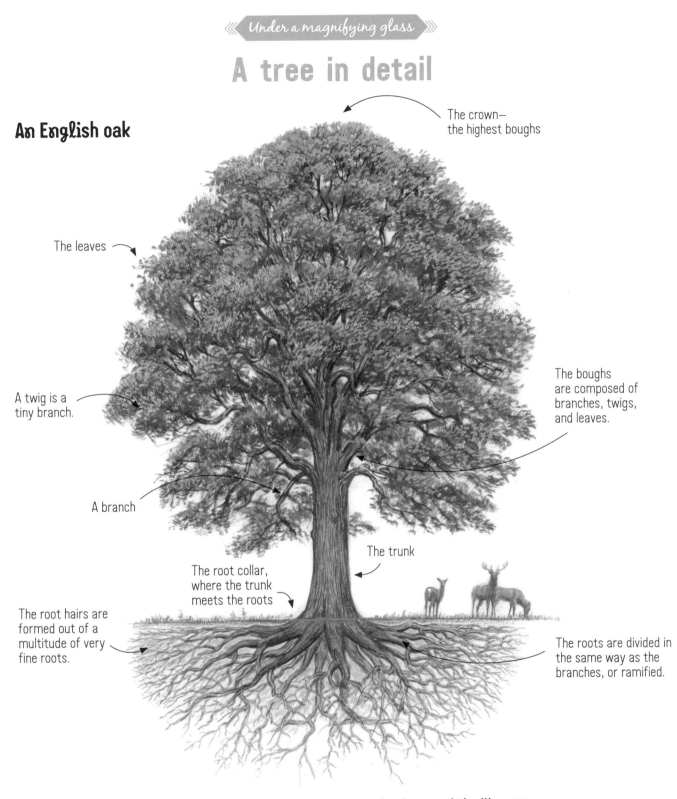

The crown—
the highest boughs

The leaves

The boughs
are composed of
branches, twigs,
and leaves.

A twig is a
tiny branch.

A branch

The trunk

The root collar,
where the trunk
meets the roots

The root hairs are
formed out of a
multitude of very
fine roots.

The roots are divided in
the same way as the
branches, or ramified.

**The boughs of each species of tree make up its characteristic silhouette.
This oak has an egg-shaped form.**

TREE TRUNKS ARE SOLID!

——≫≫≫—≪≪≪——

A trunk is sturdy. It supports the entire weight of the boughs.

Protective bark

The bark covering a tree's trunk is vital: without bark, a tree will die. Its thickness depends on the species; it protects the living part of the wood from rain, sun, cold, and attacks by animals.

Sap flows under the bark.

Sap is the lifeblood to a tree; it irrigates all parts of a tree, following two circuits:

✳ **Raw sap**, composed of water and mineral salts, rises from the roots to the crown of the tree. It flows under a thicker layer of wood.

✳ **Elaborated sap** moves down from the crown to the roots through a thin layer of wood right under the bark. It is rich in nutrients (sugars), allowing the tree to live and grow.

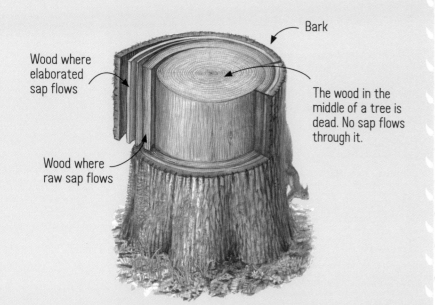

Bark

Wood where elaborated sap flows

The wood in the middle of a tree is dead. No sap flows through it.

Wood where raw sap flows

The bark changes as the trunk gets thicker.

✳ In young trees, the bark is often smooth and sometimes green.

A young silver birch

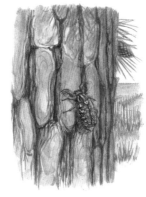

✳ In older trees, the bark thickens and turns gray or brown.

A maritime pine

✳ In some trees, the external layer of bark renews itself regularly: it falls off in plaques from plane trees and in ribbons from wild cherries and eucalyptus.

A plane tree

What is clinging to the bark?

1. A nuthatch is a bird that taps on the bark of trees in the winter to…

[a] dislodge insects and spiders.
[b] break the hazelnuts it wedged in the bark.
[c] dig a hole to nest in.

2. Mistletoe is a plant shaped like a ball that attaches to a branch to…

[a] attack the fruit.
[b] protect itself from rodents.
[c] suck the sap from a tree.

3. Moss often grows on the bark of a trunk—on which side?

[a] on the most damp side
[b] always on the north
[c] always on the south

4. Ivy is a climbing plant that clings to the bark of trees to…

[a] suck the sap from a tree.
[b] seek more light.
[c] protect the trunk.

SO MANY LEAVES!

—————⟫⟫⟫——⟪⟪⟪—————

Leaves come in many different shapes and locations, depending on the type of tree.

A leaf has two parts:

✳ The main part of a leaf is the **limb**, which is often flat and crisscrossed with **veins** through which the sap flows. Limbs have different shapes from one tree to the next: rounded, oval, palmate, or needle-shaped. And the edge can be smooth, wavy, toothed…

✳ The other part of a leaf, the **leafstalk**, can be long or short. It fastens the limb to the twig.

Two types of trees

✳ **Deciduous trees** have wide-limb leaves that can be simple or compound.

Chestnut trees have simple leaves.

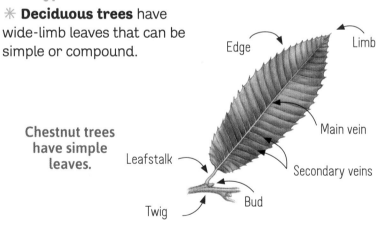

Edge
Limb
Main vein
Leafstalk
Secondary veins
Twig
Bud

✳ **Coniferous trees**, or conifers, have narrow-limb leaves with a single vein; they are needle-shaped on pines and scale-shaped on cypress trees.

A Scotch pine

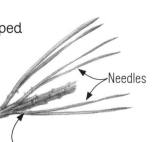

Needles

The leafstalk is very short.

Leaves can be arranged in 3 different ways.

Alternate leaves

A beech twig

These leaves grow singly at various levels on a twig.

Opposite leaves

A field maple twig

These leaves are attached facing each other on the twig.

Verticillate leaves

A juniper twig

This foliage (always needles) is attached at the same level on the twig, in clusters of 3 or more.

Simple or compound leaves?

Simple leaves have an all-in-one limb.

Compound leaf limbs come in several parts, called leaflets.

1 main vein

Edge with several rounded lobes

Short leafstalk

Oak leaf

Edge with 5 triangular lobes (or sometimes 3)

Long leafstalk

Main veins

Plane tree leaf

Smooth edge

1 main vein

Silvery underside

Short leafstalk

Olive tree leaf

1 main vein

Smooth edge

Long leafstalk

5 to 13 leaflets attached along the main vein

Locust tree leaf

Toothed edge

9 to 15 leaflets attached along the main vein

Long leafstalk

1 main vein

Ash tree leaf

Main veins

7- or sometimes 5-leaflet limb

Edge of double-toothed leaflets

Long leafstalk

Horse chestnut leaf

Find the leaves with just one main vein!

11

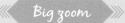
A year in the life of a tree

Conifers, which keep their needles year round, have evergreen foliage.
Deciduous trees, which lose all their leaves in the fall, have deciduous foliage.

A coniferous tree: spruce

Coniferous trees, such as spruce trees, have needle-shaped foliage
that they keep for 5 to 9 years, renewing the needles little by little.

In the summer

Spruce trees pour all their energy into making wood in their youngest twigs and forming buds for the following year.

In the fall

Old needles fall off, but the tree stays green all year long.

In the spring

This is the only season when a spruce tree grows. After starting off with buds, it unfurls new twigs, followed by new needles at the end of the twigs, and then it blooms.

In the winter

Buds are protected by scales coated with a sticky material: resin. Its needles aren't harmed by freezing, and its branches don't hold snow.

A deciduous tree: the wild cherry

Deciduous trees, such as wild cherries, have wide leaves that last only one summer. They make new ones every year.

In the summer

Wild cherry leaves are fully grown and stop growing. The tree is already forming buds at the base of its leafstalks, which will develop twigs, leaves, or flowers the following year.

In the fall

The days grow shorter. Because the leaves are no longer feeding on the sap, they dry up and fall off.

In the spring

The days grow longer. The sap begins to flow again under the bark. The buds swell; some buds sprout flowers. Then the leaves spread quickly.

In the winter

The wild cherry has lost all its leaves. It is dormant, with reserves of nutrients stored in its roots. The buds have nothing to fear from freezing; they are protected by scales.

In a park

Lebanese cedar

Silver linden

Weeping willow

Banana tree

Boxwood

My observatory

1. Which tree has silver leaves?

2. Which tree is planted in the middle of a lawn?

3. Which tree loses its bark in plaques?

4. Which tree gets clipped as a hedge?

14

London plane

Hornbeam

Horse chestnut

5. Which tree has branches that reach down to the ground?

6. Which plant that grows as high as a tree doesn't have a trunk?

7. Which large conifer has a flat crown?

8. Which kind of shrub is often clipped in a ball shape?

HOW DOES A TREE GROW?

GROWING TALLER AND SPREADING

A tree grows throughout its life, at uneven speeds.

The trunk thickens.

The wood of the tree grows in successive layers under the bark. In temperate regions, two layers of wood form every year. One wide layer grows in the spring: abundant sap rises through the wide vessels in its light-colored wood. Another, narrower one starts growing in the summer: raw sap flows slowly up through the narrow vessels in its dark wood. The trunk, branches, and roots all grow this way

Growth rings

A ring is composed of a layer of light-colored wood and a layer of dark wood. We can figure out the **age of a tree** by counting its rings. The oldest rings are located in the center, where the sap doesn't flow anymore. This very hard, dead wood supports the tree.

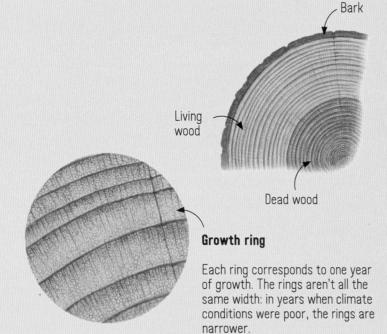

Bark

Living wood

Dead wood

Growth ring

Each ring corresponds to one year of growth. The rings aren't all the same width: in years when climate conditions were poor, the rings are narrower.

A tree grows taller.

✳ **In the summer**, buds form at the base of the leafstalk.

Terminal bud

Leafstalk

Buds

Twig

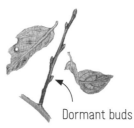

Dormant buds

✳ **In the fall**, the leaves drop

✳ **In the winter**, all that are left are the dormant buds, protected by brown scales.

✳ **In the spring**, the scales fall off the terminal bud. The branch grows longer. The buds formed the previous summer have given birth to shoots bearing new leaves.

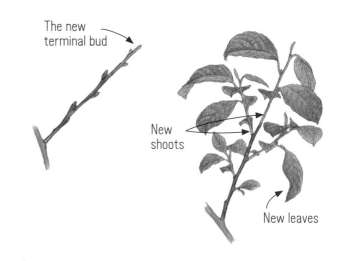

The new terminal bud

New shoots

New leaves

Measure a tree!

✳ *Figure out the height of a tree* ✳

1. Choose an isolated tree that you can see from top to bottom.
2. Take 2 straight sticks of the same length, around 8 inches (20 cm). Hold one of the sticks horizontally at eye level and the other one vertically at the far end of the first (see the diagram at right).
3. Aim the sticks at the tree. Step backward or forward until the two ends of the vertical stick match up with the base of the trunk and the crown of the tree.
4. When you are in the right position, draw a line on the ground with your foot. Then use a ruler to measure the distance between you and the tree. This will give you the height of the tree.

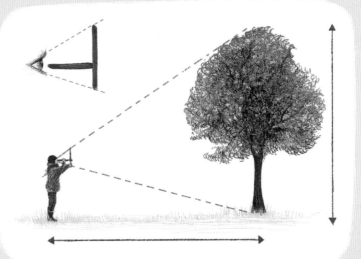

✳ *How to measure the circumference of a trunk and calculate its diameter* ✳

1. Wrap a string around the tree trunk at chest height.
2. Use a ruler to measure the length of the string to get the circumference of the trunk.

3. Divide the circumference of the trunk (in centimeters) by pi (3.14).

   For example: if the circumference of the trunk is 100 cm:

   $100 \div 3.14 = 31.84$

   The diameter of the trunk is about 32 cm, or 12.5 inches.

DRINKING THROUGH THE ROOTS

A tree needs water, lots of water!

The main role of the roots

Roots grow long to draw water from the ground. The water is absorbed at the level of the finest roots. These form the root hairs; new ones grow regularly, the way leaves do

A terrific team

Fungi live in, or on, the fine roots of trees. They help the tree absorb water loaded with mineral salts, forming the raw sap.

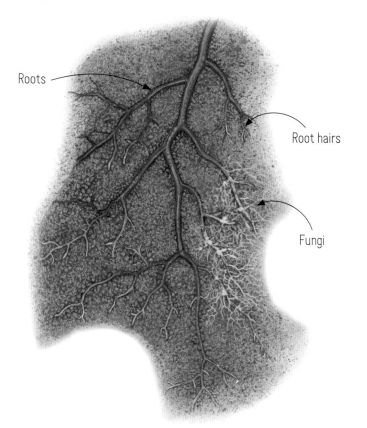

Roots

Root hairs

Fungi

Two other roles roots play

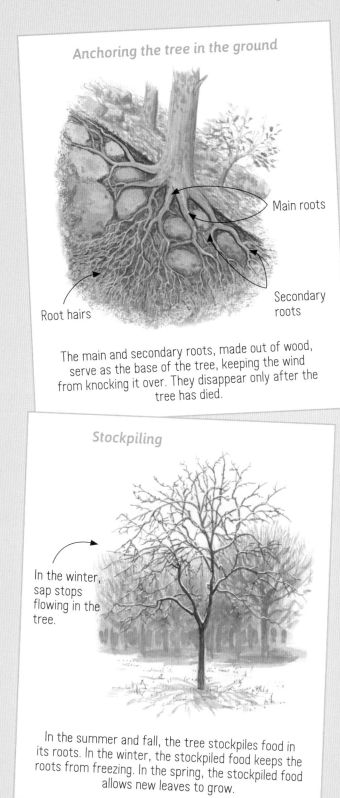

Anchoring the tree in the ground

Main roots

Root hairs

Secondary roots

The main and secondary roots, made out of wood, serve as the base of the tree, keeping the wind from knocking it over. They disappear only after the tree has died.

Stockpiling

In the winter, sap stops flowing in the tree.

In the summer and fall, the tree stockpiles food in its roots. In the winter, the stockpiled food keeps the roots from freezing. In the spring, the stockpiled food allows new leaves to grow.

Four types of roots

Roots change shape, depending on the tree's species, its age,
and the obstacles they meet in the ground.

Pivoting roots

These grow out from the
main root, from which they
pivot and plunge deep into
the ground.

Oblique roots

These grow into the
ground from all the sides
of the root collar.

Beech

Root collar

Lateral roots

These spread horizontally.
They sometimes grow out
of the ground.

Spruce

Roots with nodules

These pair with fungi and
bacteria, forming nodules
that feed the tree so it can
grow in poor soil.

Alder

Nodules

EATING WITH THE LEAVES

The tree prepares its own food in its green leaves.

Basic ingredients

To feed itself, a tree absorbs the gas **carbon dioxide** (CO_2), from the air. It enters the green leaves through tiny slits, called **stomates**. The tree also draws **water** (H_2O), from the ground, which is absorbed through the roots and then routed to the leaves in the **raw sap** flowing through the living wood.

How does it work?

The tree makes its food during the day because it needs energy from sunlight to assemble the carbon dioxide and water in its leaves. This is called **photosynthesis**. It then assembles sugars, which, in **elaborated sap**, will feed all parts of the tree, along with water and dioxygen (O_2), which the leaves expel.

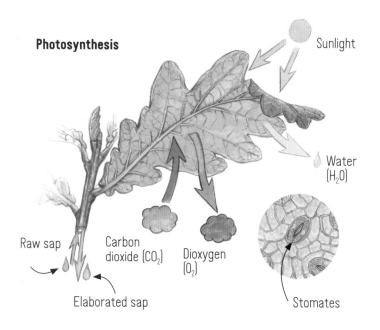

Photosynthesis

Sunlight

Water (H_2O)

Raw sap

Carbon dioxide (CO_2)

Dioxygen (O_2)

Elaborated sap

Stomates

The importance of photosynthesis

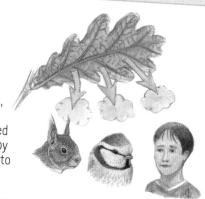

During photosynthesis, a tree expels dioxygen (O_2), used for **respiration** by all living beings, into the air.

Trees are not the only living things to undergo photosynthesis. On the surface of oceans, **phytoplankton** produce half the dioxygen we breathe on Earth.

Phytoplankton

(O_2)

(CO_2)

(CO_2)

(CO_2)

(O_2)

(O_2)

Trees breathe both day and night: they consume dioxygen (O_2) and expel carbon dioxide (CO_2). But during the day, thanks to photosynthesis, they produce more O_2 than they consume and they absorb more CO_2 than they expel. In this way, they improve the composition of our air and control the **Earth's climates**.

Everything about how a tree grows

1. When a tree grows, a swing hanging from its branch…

a gets higher.

b gets lower.

c stays at the same height.

2. To grow, a tree needs…

a water.

b water and light.

c water, air, and light.

3. A tree makes its food in…

a its green leaves.

b its wood.

c its bark.

4. To absorb water, a tree…

a pairs its roots with fungi.

b sends its roots toward a stream.

c captures rain with its leaves.

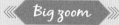

Trees know how to defend themselves.

When trees are attacked, they can't scream or run away, but they do know how to protect themselves and take care of themselves.

Trees protect themselves.

Prickly leaves

Holly has spikes on the edges of its leaves. Animals avoid biting these leaves to keep from hurting themselves. But on top of its crown, out of the reach of herbivores, holly grows flat leaves without spikes.

Toxic substances

Yews produce a poison in their leaves, branches, bark, and seeds. Only the flesh of their fruit is not toxic, and birds eat it. But if a careless herbivore nibbles on the foliage, it gets so sick, it will never try again.

Thorns

Black locust trees repel herbivores with the very pointy thorns on their branches.

Trees take care of themselves.

A protective repair

Some insects lay their eggs on leaves. To defend itself, a tree creates a wrapping called a gall around the egg. This way, the larva feeds off the gall instead of nibbling the leaf.

A useful scar

If one of its big branches breaks off, a tree heals its injury by producing a special wood that forms a kind of fold that keeps diseases from rotting the tree.

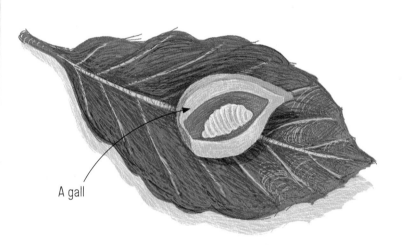

A gall

A useful ointment

When insects attack the bark of a cherry tree to suck on its sap, fungi or bacteria can get into the tree and might destroy its wood. So a cherry tree makes a sticky gum to treat its wound.

Sticky gum

In a temperate forest

Scotch pine

Littleleaf linden

Hazelnut tree

Beech tree

My observatory

1. Which shrub grows at the edge of a forest?

2. On which tree is the jay sitting?

3. Which tree doesn't let anything grow at its base?

4. In which tree does a woodpecker dig its nest?

Silver birch

Spruce

English oak

Holly

5. Which tree has orange bark?

6. Under which tree is the squirrel shelling a cone?

7. Which tree has silvery white bark?

8. Which tree forms a prickly bush?

THE BIRTH OF
A TREE

TO EACH ITS OWN SEED

A tree generally starts off as a seed. Before becoming a giant, it emerges from the ground as a thin stem!

Everything is already in the seed.

A seed holds the **embryo** that will turn into a tree, along with the food it will need, all stored in the **cotyledons**. A hard coating keeps it safe.

The embryo

The 2 cotyledons

The seed coat

The acorn holds the oak seed.

How some deciduous trees germinate

1. In the spring, when the soil is warm and moist enough, the seed swells with water and the embryo wakes up: it produces its first root, tearing the seed coat and plunging into the ground to drink water.

2. Then, a stem rises skyward.

3. The first green leaves appear so the tiny tree can eat. Its cotyledons are empty.

Birth of a young oak

When an acorn sprouts, the cotyledons remain underground.

① ② ③

Two other ways that trees germinate

Deciduous trees

The first leaves

When a seed germinates, the cotyledons are lifted out of the ground along with the stem. They don't stay underground. Because they're green, they can be confused with the leaves.

The cotyledons

Birth of a young beech tree

Conifers

4. Then the first tufts of needles appear.

3. When the cotyledons emerge from the seed coat, they form a star.

2. It bears several cotyledons.

1. The young stem emerges from the seed.

Birth of a young spruce

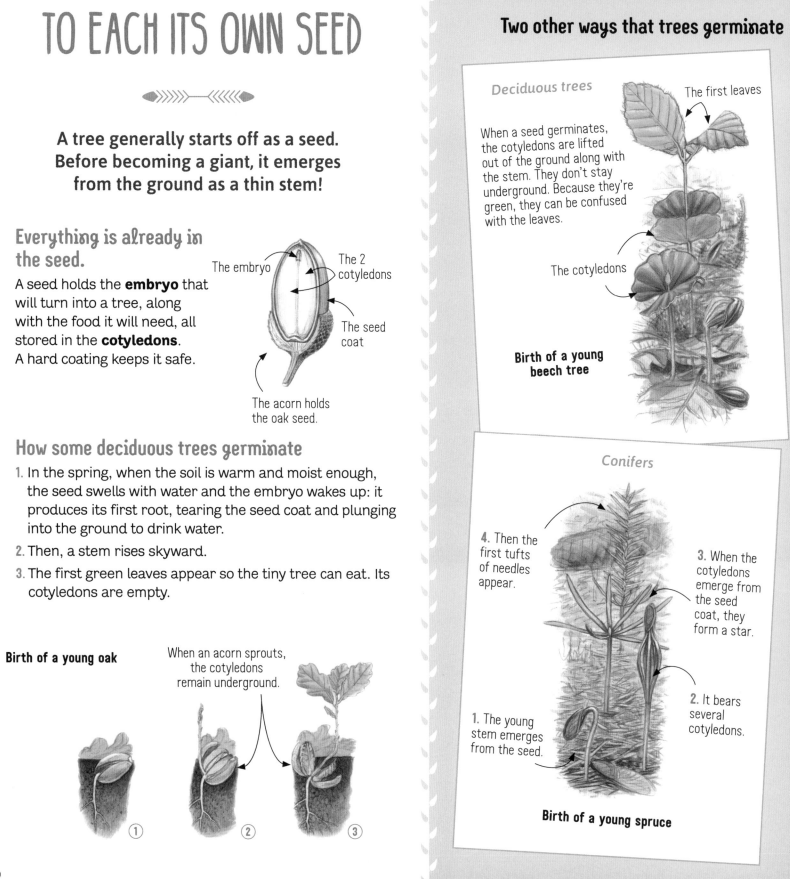

Traveling seeds

How do seeds germinate far from the tree that produced them?

Some seeds fly.

Field elm seeds are surrounded by a round, lightweight wing that enables the wind to carry them.

Some seeds roll.

The **horse chestnut**'s seed is big and round. It is covered by a smooth shell and rolls on the ground.

Some seeds float.

The slender seeds of the **alder** use their little floaters to travel across the surface of a body of water without sinking.

Some seeds are carried by animals.

The spotted nutcracker loves **Swiss pine** seeds. It collects them and hides them in the ground. The ones it doesn't eat germinate.

Beech tree seeds have prickly seed coats that grab hold of an animal's fur, such as a wild boar— an effective way to get around!

Foxes eat **wild cherries** and **elderberries** that have dropped to the ground. When the seeds emerge from the droppings, they are ready to germinate!

A fox's dropping

THE ROLE OF FLOWERS

All trees bloom once they reach adulthood. Sometimes their flowers are so discreet or high up that they aren't noticeable.

Reproduction

A tree uses the sexual organs located in its flowers to reproduce. **Stamens** are the male organs that contain the **pollen**. The female organ is the **pistil**, which holds an **ovule**.

Male and/or female flowers?

✳ With some trees, such as the linden and the horse chestnut, the male and female organs are included in the same flower.

Pistil

Stamens

A wild cherry flower

✳ With other types of trees, such as oaks and all the conifers, some trees have male flowers and others have female flowers.

Hazelnut flowers

The male flowers form hanging clusters called catkins.

The female flowers are inconspicuous.

> **How do flowers produce seeds?**
> Whatever the tree and its type of flower, the pollen grains (male) land on the pistil (female) of another flower in the same species. This is **pollination**. A fertile pollen grain then fertilizes an ovule, and an embryo forms. This process of **fertilization** is how every fertilized ovule becomes a seed!

How does the pollen reach the pistil of a flower in its own species?

✳ *On the wind*
The pollen of male flowers is carried by the wind to the female flowers on another tree.

European larch flowers

Pollen

A female flower

A male flower

After they are fertilized, female flowers grow into cones that hold the seeds.

✳ *By insects*
Insects are attracted by the colors and scent of flowers. When they forage, pollen grains latch onto their bodies. When they land on another flower, the pollen grains fall onto the pistil.

Horse chestnut flowers

Only the fertilized flowers will produce horse chestnuts.

Trees with two different sexes

With hollies (as well as willows, poplars, and ginkgo), a tree is either male or female.

Male holly flower

Female holly flower

A bee carries pollen from a male holly…

…to a female holly

1. On **male hollies**, all the flowers have 4 stamens that release the pollen. The pistil is not developed. On **female hollies**, all the flowers have a large central pistil. The tiny stamens don't have any pollen.

2. The white, fragrant male flowers of holly attract insects to carry the pollen from a male tree to a female one.

3. Once fertilized, the female flowers produce fruit: these are the little red balls that hold the seeds.

4. Birds eat the fruit of the holly, then scatter the seeds by spitting them out or getting rid of them in their droppings. When they germinate, they give birth to a male or a female tree.

ANOTHER WAY TO REPRODUCE

—⟫⟫—⟪⟪—

Sometimes, trees reproduce without using flowers or seeds. This is called asexual reproduction.

A fast method

When trees multiply without making seeds, they use less energy and occupy an area faster. But because these individual trees are located very close to one another and are identical, they have less of a chance of surviving when the climate changes.

Starting from a branch

Some trees, such as hollies and cedars, reproduce from their flowers and seeds, as well as their branches. When their long, flexible branches reach the ground, they develop roots. Then the end of the branch straightens up and produces a young tree.

Holly

Starting from dormant buds

On locusts and lilacs, buds develop on a root near the ground's surface. A new stem grows: it produces roots and becomes independent. This is called a **sucker**.

Sucker

Lilac

What is a graft?

Gardeners have invented a technique for growing trees that produce bigger, more numerous fruit: this is called grafting.

✳ When an apple seed germinates, it produces a tree with vigorous roots, but its fruit tend to be small.

✳ When the young tree is well rooted, the gardener cuts off its crown and makes a slit to slip in a branch taken from another apple tree that produces good apples.

✳ If the graft takes, the raw sap from the roots will feed the new branch and produce great fruit.

Grow a tree!

✳ **Sow seeds** ✳

1. In the fall, gather horse chestnuts, maple seeds, or acorns. Choose the nicest ones.

3. Put the tub in the bottom of the refrigerator. The seeds need to be cold to germinate.

2. Fill a little tub with damp sand and bury the seeds in it.

4. One to two months later, take the seeds out and put them in a pot under 1.2 to 1.6 inches (3 to 4 cm) of dirt. Water them regularly. Be patient. They can take a month to germinate.

✳ **Take a cutting** ✳

1. At the end of winter, cut off the end of a very straight willow branch that is more than 32 inches (80 cm) long.

2. Push it at least 16 inches (40 cm) deep into damp dirt. Make sure the buds are at the top.

3. Water it regularly. Roots will develop in the dirt, and leaves will appear very soon.

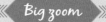
The life of a tree

A tree can live for decades, even hundreds of years. Some can even reappear.

From birth to old age

1. A quick start

In the spring, a seed soaks up water. It germinates within a few days.

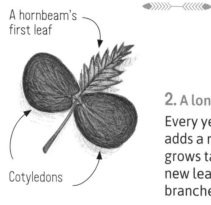

A hornbeam's first leaf

Cotyledons

2. A long youth

Every year, the young tree adds a ring to its trunk and grows taller. Every spring, new leaves appear on new branches.

New leaves

During the winter, a hornbeam often keeps its withered leaves.

3. Adulthood

When a tree reaches its adult size (it takes around 20 years for a hornbeam), it stops growing. It blooms for the first time. Then, its flowers produce seeds.

In the fall, a hornbeam's female flowers produce garlands of seeds.

A hornbeam blooms when it is about 20 years old. It measures around 33 feet (10 m) tall.

4. Peaceful old age

As a tree ages, it produces fewer and fewer roots, leaves, and seeds. It grows shorter and shorter branches, its top branches die, and its crown flattens.

Crown

The end of a tree

❋❯❯❯❯—❮❮❮❮❖

* A tree dies slowly (unless it is diseased). Its sap stops flowing, and it loses all its leaves…but it can remain standing for several years.

A hornbeam can live 100 to 150 years.

* Once a dead tree has fallen to the ground, decomposers, such as earthworms and fungi, attack its wood, and it rots. In this way, its fertile components are returned to the soil and other plants can use them.

A fallen hornbeam can take 10 to 20 years to completely disappear.

Rebirth

❯❯❯❯—❮❮❮❮

* When the trunk of certain deciduous trees is cut, new branches grow on the stump. These sprouts are all identical.

Sprouts on stump, 1 year after the stump was cut

Stump

* The sprouts form young stems, which are still fed by the tree's roots. They grow quickly, but they will never get as big as the original tree's trunk.

Sprouts on stump, 25 years after the stump was cut

In an orchard

Olive tree

Fig tree

Pear tree

Quince tree

My Observatory

1. Which tree was pruned to take advantage of the warmth of the wall?

2. Which tree was pruned to spread horizontally?

3. Which tree produces fruit called quince?

4. Which tree has a very tall trunk?

Almond tree

Cherry tree

Apricot tree

Apple tree

5. Which tree will product orange-fleshed fruit?

6. What do you call a tree that produces almonds?

7. Which tree grows fruit that produce oil?

8. Which fruit tree is a big bush?

THE POWERS OF TREES

CHAMPIONS OF ADAPTATION

Like all living creatures, a tree needs to be able to tell what is happening around it and react if necessary. How does it do that?

The secret of trees

A tree doesn't have brains or a heart. Its vital functions are spread among its leaves, its trunk, and its roots. Thanks to this **dispersed organization**, a tree is less likely to lose any vital organ if a predator attacks it.

Leaves with multiple uses

A tree can have thousands of leaves. Each leaf serves as the tree's eyes, intestines, and lungs. Like eyes, they detect where light is coming from and face the light to capture it. A tree's food is assimilated in its leaves, similar to how our intestines work. And it is in the leaves that exchanges with air take place, as in our lungs.

Sensitive roots

A tree can have billions of small growths on its roots. Each root hair serves as the tree's ears and hands to explore the ground. They use them to perceive water noises and grow in that direction.

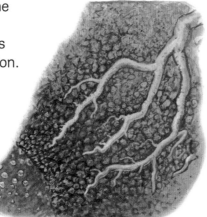

Three great powers

Retaining and feeding the soil

Tree roots hold back the soil that could be washed away by rain. When they decompose, dead leaves produce compost, a natural fertilizer.

Refreshing and watering

In the summer, a leaf transpires as many as 50 gallons (200 l) of water every day. Trees accumulate water in their leaves and expel part of it, helping to freshen the air and maybe even making it rain.

Purifying the atmosphere

During photosynthesis, trees capture carbon dioxide (CO_2) from the air and retain it in their wood, reducing the atmosphere's amount of CO_2, which is responsible for global warming. Their foliage filters fine particles (hazardous to our lungs) and absorbs certain polluting gases.

Trees stand up to any test.

When a tree starts growing on a slope, it can straighten itself vertically as it keeps on growing.

European larch

Conifers living by the sea develop branches and leaves that are protected from the wind.

Maritime pine

When deer graze on the crowns of young firs, the side branches lengthen to reshape them.

Silver fir

Because growing roots exert such incredible pressure, a tree can raise the paving of sidewalks!

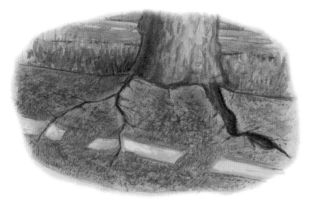

Plane tree

Over time, a tree can swallow a gate, post, or cable leaning against its trunk: little by little, its bark covers the object trapped in the wood.

Locust tree

43

LUMBER MAKERS

Trees can produce materials humans aren't able to make.

Wood, a superb raw material

Every species of tree produces wood in different colors and structures. The more slowly a tree grows, the more compact and heavy its wood becomes. Woodworkers use dead wood from the middle of a trunk because it is sturdier.

How it is harvested

Wood is harvested from a tree as soon as it stops growing. After it gets cut down, the branches are removed and the trunk is transported to a sawmill. There, it is dried, treated for insects and fungi, and sawed into boards. The branches are used for heating or shredded to make paper and cardboard, among other things.

Tree products

✳ Resin
Resin is harvested from a pine tree by cutting its bark. It is used to manufacture drugs and paint.

A tree makes resin to heal its wounds. Resin is not sap.

✳ Cork
The bark on a cork oak is harvested every 10 years. Cork is an excellent insulator against noise and cold. It is also used to make bottle stoppers.

✳ Branches
Ash and elm branches, which are especially fast growing, are used for heating. Their foliage feeds livestock.

Pollarded trees are trees whose branches get cut every 6 to 15 years.

The wood around you

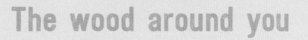

1. To build a piece of furniture, people use…

a the trunk.
b the branches.
c the roots.

2. Matches are usually made of…

a fir wood.
b oak wood.
c poplar wood.

3. The ties supporting train tracks are…

a iron.
b massive oak.
c plastic.

4. Paper fibers can be recycled…

a once.
b 5 times.
c indefinitely.

PRODUCERS OF FRUIT

><>>>———<<<<

All trees produce fruit, but not all fruit is edible by humans.

Where does fruit come from?

The fruit of a tree is formed from a pollinated flower. It contains a seed or seeds in pulp protected by an outer skin.

An edible seed coat

Some fruit, like that of pear, apple, plum, and orange trees, has seeds in its core, surrounded by a juicy pulp that we can eat.

Pear pulp holds 10 seeds.

Seeds to nibble on

With other fruit, like that of walnut, hazelnut, almond and chestnut trees, it's the seed itself we eat. It has to be removed from a shell that is sometimes as hard as wood and inedible.

A walnut is the fruit of the walnut tree.

Flowers and leaves are harvested, too.

＊Herbal tea is made with linden tree flowers, gathered when they are in full bloom—that is, right before they become fruit.

A linden flower

＊In the tropics, the young leaves of tea bushes are used to make various kinds of tea.

A leaf from a tea bush

＊Rosemary, laurel, sage, and thyme leaves are used in cooking to flavor our dishes while cooking.

Evergreen **rosemary** is harvested all year long.

＊Cypress tree cones, eucalyptus and ash leaves, willow bark, and pine and fir tree buds are used to make medications.

Cypress tree fruit is harvested while unripe to make a remedy known to improve circulation.

Animals that feed on trees

Leaf eaters

Butterfly caterpillars feed on leaves.

Every species of butterfly has its favorite tree. For example, a **silkworm**, which is the mulberry caterpillar, feeds on the leaves of the white mulberry.

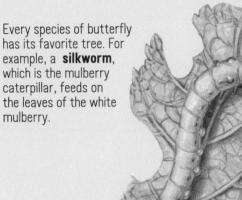

Fruit eaters

Scarlet fruit attract birds to a tree.

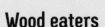

Robins love the fruit of the European spindle.

Seed eaters

Rodents often gather seeds from the ground.

Mice nibble on acorns, hazelnuts, and cherry pits found at the foot of trees.

Wood eaters

Beetle larvae, such as those of great capricorn beetles, grow for 6 months while gnawing on wood.

The **great capricorn beetle larva** hatches under bark, then digs deeper to feed itself before emerging to take flight.

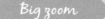
»»» Incredible gifts ««««

By studying trees, scientists have learned lots of amazing things about how they live.
And there's still a lot to discover!

Trees communicate among themselves.

✳ They send messages through the air…

In South Africa, scientists observed how an acacia reacted to an antelope when it came to graze on its leaves:

• As soon as the antelope started grazing, the tree produced a toxic substance that made its foliage indigestible.

• The antelope then stopped grazing and headed for another acacia.

• But the first acacia released a gas in the air that alerted the other acacias. Their leaves then became toxic before the antelope even attacked them!

✳ …or underground.

A tree with diseased foliage produces substances that flow down to its roots. The fungi in contact with the roots then launch a warning to other trees (whether or not they are in the same species), helping them to protect themselves.

Trees help each other.

---

* Large trees cast shadows over their young shoots to protect them from sunburn. Then, when the shoots need light to grow, they compete with each other: the most powerful ones stifle and kill the more delicate ones. Only the most vigorous shoots will grow into big trees.

* In the tropical forest, where the sun has trouble penetrating the canopy, the leaves on big trees keep their distance from one another. Each one is aware of its neighbors' presence and avoids casting shadows on them.

* When a tree is cut down, its neighbors provide a little food to its stump through their roots, because it no longer has any foliage with which to feed itself. This helps the stump heal: it doesn't rot, and it slowly builds a protective wood and bark covering.

In the Mediterranean countryside

Holm oak

Montpellier maple

Parasol pine

Burning bush

My Observatory

1. Which leafy tree keeps its leaves in winter?

2. Which coniferous tree has russet cones?

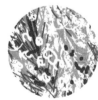

3. Which shrub is covered with white flowers in winter?

4. Which shrub bears fruit and flowers at the same time?

Aleppo pine

Mediterranean cypress

Arbutus

Tree heather

5. Which little leafy tree loses its leaves before winter?

6. Which large tree has a crown spread out like a parasol?

7. Which shrub is covered in bright-red fruit in winter?

8. Which tree stands upright like a letter "I"?

MAGNIFICENT
TREES

Record-breaking trees

Magnolia
The magnolia has the biggest flowers of any tree: they can measure up to 8 inches (20 cm) in diameter.

Jackfruit
This tree, a native of India and Bangladesh, bears the biggest fruit: some jackfruit weigh more than 55 pounds (25 kg).

Evergreen sequoia
This United States West Coast conifer is one of the biggest trees in the world. Some reach a height of 375 feet (115 m).

Cork oak
This deciduous evergreen tree produces the thickest bark of any tree. It is harvested for making corks.

King's holly

This is the oldest tree in the world—at least 43,000 years old. It has pretty flowers but does not produce any fruit or seeds. Its branches take root and form a perpetually self-renewing bush.

Baobab

This tree grows mostly in Africa and has the biggest trunk of any tree: some are as big around as 80 feet (25 m). It takes 20 people holding hands to reach around it.

Welwitschia

This desert tree's trunk grows under the surface of the sand. It has only two leaves, which twist along the ground to as long as 13 feet (4 m), fraying at the ends into multiple sections.

Ginkgo biloba

Native to China, this is one of the oldest trees in the world: its ancestors were growing on Earth well before the age of the dinosaurs.

Banyan

This tree, native to South Asia, has the most developed branches of any tree: supported by air roots, these branches can cover an area as large as 2.5 acres (1 ha).

Deciduous trees

European larch

This mountain conifer is the only European deciduous conifer. It has needle-shaped foliage. Its fruit are little cones that stay on the tree for 2 to 3 years.

Montpellier maple

In the spring, this tree's little flowers form bouquets at the tip of its branches. They often come out before the leaves and attract bees.

Black mulberry

This little tree is grown for its delicious black mulberry fruit.
Don't mix them up with blackberries (just as good), which grow on wild, prickly blackberry bushes.

Downy oak

This tree likes warm, dry climates. The truffle, a fungus highly prized by gastronomes, colonizes its roots.

Ash

It produces amazing fruit called samaras. They are dry and flat, with a little wing, and they hang in a cluster on the tree all winter long.

Hackberry

This tree is often planted along streets. Its gray bark cracks with age. Its fruit look like cherries, but their flesh is tasteless.

Pussy willow

The male catkins on this willow are big, silky, and yellow. As with all willows, male and female flowers grow on different trees.

Walnut

It can grow as high as 65 feet (20 m). It is grown for its wood, which is used to make furniture, and its fruit, walnuts.

Sycamore maple

The sycamore is the biggest maple tree; it can get as tall as 100 feet (30 m). As with other maple trees, its fruit are 2-wing samaras.

Chestnut

This tree lives in forests. Its trunk can be huge and grows hollow with age. Its edible fruit, chestnuts, come in groups of 2 or 3 inside a prickly husk, called a bur.

Evergreen trees

English yew

This conifer does not produce resin, emit a scent, or produce any cones. The female tree bears plump berries called arils.

Arbutus

Also called a strawberry tree, it does not get taller than 30 feet (9 m). It has foliage all year long. At the beginning of winter, it bears flowers and ripe fruit at the same time.

Common juniper

The common juniper has short, prickly needles. Only the female flowering shrubs produce fruit: juniper berries, which take 3 years to ripen.

Blue gum eucalyptus

This tree, a native of Australia, is grown in Mediterranean regions. Its leaves give off a scent, its flowers don't have petals, and its fruit are bluish gray.

Olive

The trunk of this Mediterranean tree becomes crooked and knotty with age. Its flower clusters produce fruit with a pit: olives.

Parasol pine

This tree gets its name from its high crown, flattened in the shape of a parasol. Its cone can contain as many as 100 edible seeds: pine nuts.

Arborvitae

This tree grows slowly, to as high as 65 feet (20 m). Its tiny, scaly leaves cover the whole branch, and its cones are very tiny.

Maritime pine

This resin-producing conifer has very long needles that last 3 years.

Douglas fir

This American conifer has needles that smell like lemongrass. It grows fast and high, and it is cultivated for its wood.

Holm oak

This oak with evergreen foliage bears both male and female flowers at the same time. Only the female flowers produce fruit, called acorns.

Ornamental trees

Lebanese cedar

Tall and majestic, the Lebanese cedar can be recognized by its sturdy trunk and long, almost horizontal branches. It can live more than 1,500 years.

Copper beech

In the summer, this beech's leaves are colored by a dark-red pigment that hides its green chlorophyll.

Weeping willow

The weeping willow has slender leaves and long, supple branches that hang down to the ground. It doesn't grow from a seed: it is grown from cuttings or by grafting.

Tulip tree

This tree is native to North America. Its flowers look like large, orange tulips.

Crepe myrtle

An Asian native, the crepe myrtle is prized for its large clusters of pink flowers. It has dense foliage that turns bright red in the fall.

Boxwood

This evergreen shrub can reach a height of 20 feet (6 m) in the forest. In gardens, it is usually pruned in decorative shapes.

Empress tree

This majestic tree reaches a height of more than 50 feet (15 m). It is spectacular when it is covered with mauve flowers in the spring.

Southern catalpa

This tree is often found in public gardens and squares. Its huge leaves are heart-shaped, and its fruit are long pods that hang on the tree all winter long.

Sweetgum

In the fall, this tree's leaves turn from green to red, orange, and purple before turning brown and falling off.

Judas tree

The Judas tree's clusters of pink flowers open directly on its branches or trunk before its leaves appear.

Surprising trees

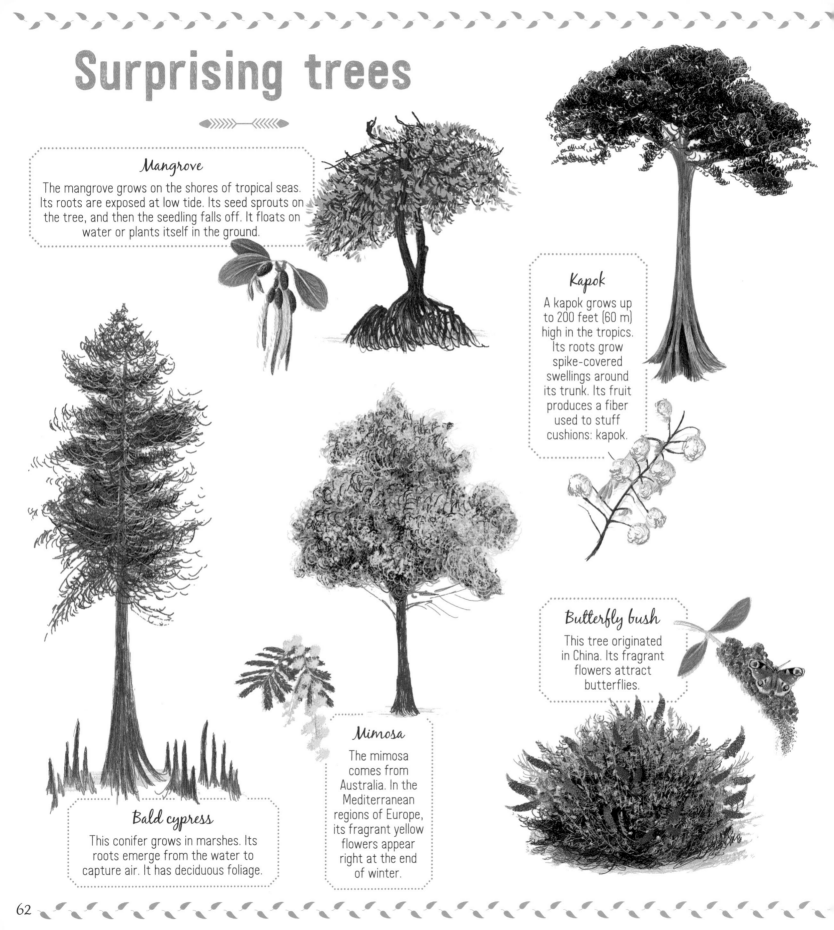

Mangrove

The mangrove grows on the shores of tropical seas. Its roots are exposed at low tide. Its seed sprouts on the tree, and then the seedling falls off. It floats on water or plants itself in the ground.

Kapok

A kapok grows up to 200 feet (60 m) high in the tropics. Its roots grow spike-covered swellings around its trunk. Its fruit produces a fiber used to stuff cushions: kapok.

Butterfly bush

This tree originated in China. Its fragrant flowers attract butterflies.

Mimosa

The mimosa comes from Australia. In the Mediterranean regions of Europe, its fragrant yellow flowers appear right at the end of winter.

Bald cypress

This conifer grows in marshes. Its roots emerge from the water to capture air. It has deciduous foliage.

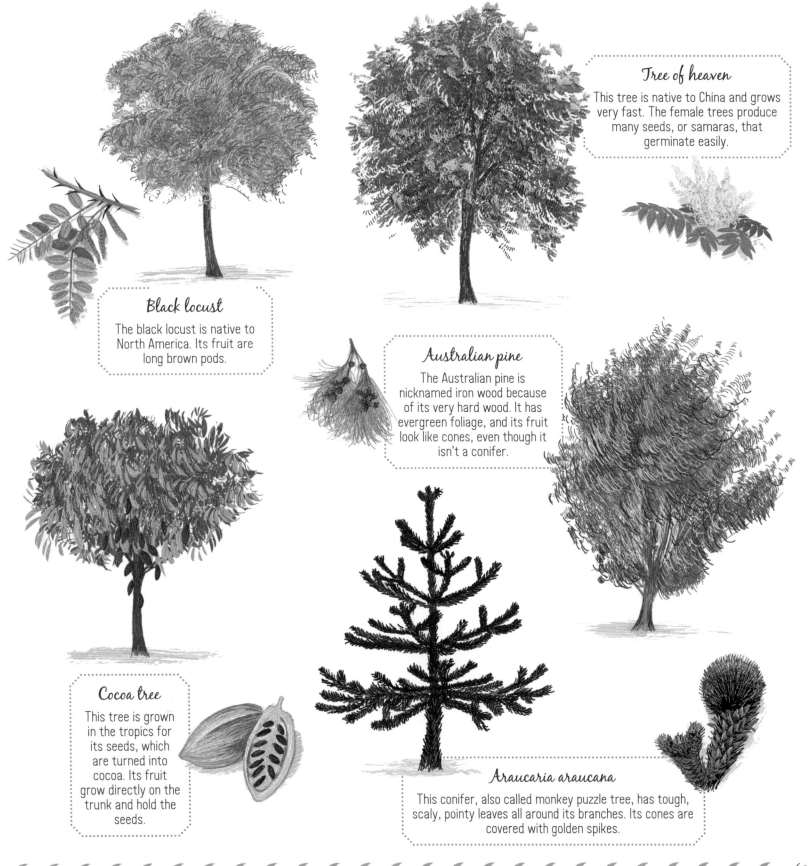

Tree of heaven
This tree is native to China and grows very fast. The female trees produce many seeds, or samaras, that germinate easily.

Black locust
The black locust is native to North America. Its fruit are long brown pods.

Australian pine
The Australian pine is nicknamed iron wood because of its very hard wood. It has evergreen foliage, and its fruit look like cones, even though it isn't a conifer.

Cocoa tree
This tree is grown in the tropics for its seeds, which are turned into cocoa. Its fruit grow directly on the trunk and hold the seeds.

Araucaria araucana
This conifer, also called monkey puzzle tree, has tough, scaly, pointy leaves all around its branches. Its cones are covered with golden spikes.

Fruit to snack on

Can you find the trees these fruits grow on in the book?

1. Arbutus berries

This fruit has skin covered with tiny points and takes a year to ripen.

2. Black mulberry

Pick this fruit when it is perfectly ripe and eat it immediately!

3. Cocoa pod

This tropical fruit holds seeds that can be transformed into chocolate.

4. Hazelnut

This dry fruit is highly appreciated by rodents such as squirrels, who store it to eat in the winter.

5. Cherry

Depending on the species, cherries can be red, black, or even yellow.

6. Walnut

This high-energy fruit is a great, quick snack.

7. Chestnut

The prickly husk of this fruit opens when ripe and releases its edible seeds.

8. Pear

There are more than 2,000 varieties of this fruit, which is harvested only in temperate countries.

9. Jackfruit

This huge tropical fruit grows only on the old branches or the trunk of the tree.

10. Apple

Its seeds contain poison... but in such small amounts it is completely harmless!

Index

ANSWERS TO GAMES

« Introducing the trees »

P. 9 Quiz: 1b, 2c, 3a, 4b
P. 11: Oak, locust, olive, and
ash leaves
PP. 14–15 My observatory:
1. Silver linden 2. Horse chestnut
3. London plane 4. Hornbeam
5. Weeping willow 6. Banana tree
7. Lebanese cedar 8. Boxwood

« How does a tree grow? »

P. 23 Quiz: 1c, 2c, 3a, 4a
PP. 26–27 My observatory:
1. Hazelnut tree 2. English oak
3. Beech tree 4. Littleleaf linden
5. Scotch pine 6. Spruce 7. Silver birch
8. Holly

«The birth of a tree»

PP. 38–39 My observatory:
1. Pear tree 2. Apple tree
3. Quince tree 4. Cherry tree
5. Apricot tree 6. Almond tree
7. Olive tree 8. Fig tree

« The powers of trees »

P. 45 Quiz: 1a, 2c, 3b, 4b
PP. 50–51 My observatory:
1. Holm oak 2. Aleppo pine 3. Tree
heather 4. Arbutus 5. Montpellier
maple 6. Parasol pine 7. Burning bush
8. Mediterranean cypress

«Fruit to snack on»

P. 64: 1. Arbutus: p. 51 or 58
2. Black mulberry: p. 56
3. Cocoa tree: p. 63
4. Hazelnut tree: p. 6 or 26
5. Cherry tree: p. 38
6. Walnut tree: p. 21 or 57
7. Chestnut tree: p. 57
8. Pear tree: p. 38
9. Jackfruit: p. 54
10. Apple tree: p. 39

Olive tree

Mangrove

Holly flowers

Weeping willow

Arborvitae

Evergreen sequoia